Radford, Hys< and The F
on old picture postcards

Grenville Jennings

OLD RADFORD CHURCH, NOTTINGHAM

1. This 'Peveril' series postcard of old Radford Church was posted on 23rd December 1904, conveying seasonal greetings from Jas Linthwaite, Radford grocer, to a gentleman in Attenborough.

Designed and Published by
Reflections of a Bygone Age,
Keyworth, Nottingham
1995
Reprinted 1999

£3.50

INTRODUCTION

As we approach the millennium, it is with great diffidence that many of us look over our shoulder into the past and wonder what life was like in our respective town or village at the turn of the century. For those who do share this feeling of how our forefathers lived and how our respective suburb looked in those early days we must thank the publishers of the picture postcard.

The areas chosen for this particular nostalgic trip into the past are Radford, Hyson Green and The Forest. Most readers will be familiar with the latter, but to others an insight into earlier life in Radford and Hyson Green may prove of interest – and to residents provide sheer blissful memories.

Geographically, the area covered is that on the west of Ilkeston Road, Alfreton Road down to Bobbers Mill, across to Sherwood Rise and down as far as Western Boulevard – though the border with Lenton over the years has always seemed somewhat negotiable! Indeed, under orders of the Local Government Board in 1880, 177 acres of land at Hyson Green, previously in the Lenton parish, were transferred to Radford, and lands in Radford were transferred to Lenton, Ilkeston Road becoming the boundary line between the two parishes.

Picture postcards were first published in Britain in 1894, but it was not until a decade later that they began to take off, when in 1902 the Post Office allowed a message to be written on the address side. This meant that the whole of one side was available for the picture, which obviously gave more scope to the publishers of postcards.

Photographic viewcards became very popular and the postcard provided the most important way of communicating news or messages in much the same way as the telephone is used today. The years up to 1914 were the 'Golden Age' of picture postcards, when millions of cards portraying every imaginable subject were published by a host of national and local firms. Hardly a village or hamlet was not documented at that time by a postcard publisher, though sometimes the number of cards available was unrelated to the size of a community.

Views of Nottingham City centre, the Castle, Arboretum and Trent Bridge were profusely covered by the publishing giants, Valentine of Dundee, Raphael Tuck and W.H. Smith as to be quite common, but for areas such as Radford and Hyson Green it was mainly local publishers such as Albert Hindley, 'Peveril' Series, W.H. Smith, 'Rex' Series and amateur photographers on whom we must rely for our glimpse into the past.

Albert Hindley was the most prolific local publisher around 1905, working from his stationery shop in Clumber Street, Nottingham (currently occupied by Granada TV Rentals). He published cards in the 'Clumber' Series, covering most of Nottingham and the surrounding area. These cards were printed in colour by a firm in Glasgow, though postcards were printed later as black and white real photographs.

Another exceptionally fine publisher was C. & A.G. Lewis, whose photographic cards were published nationally, but with a good local cross-section of cards, mostly in the 1920's.

In the main, most cards produced were of well-known locations and main thoroughfares. There are many exceptions to the rule and when a view of a side street or a local event is discovered, then the pleasure to the collector is immeasurable. One negative factor is that many of the cards produced show relatively empty streets. Indeed it was sometimes only with the help of local children that the photographer was able to provide some animation.

The views themselves provide endless fascination, with a further bonus of the message on the back. We must thank those early pioneers who produced a fascinating and accurate record of the era, and all those people who preserved the cards for us to enjoy some ninety years later.

Grenville Jennings
March 1995

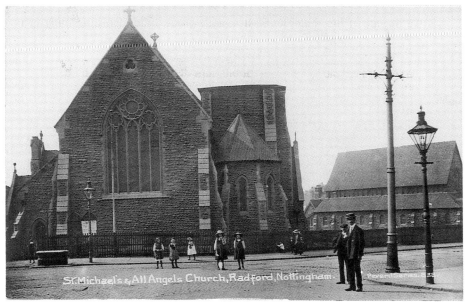

2. St. Michael's and All Angels Church in Radford. This was built in 1889 and is shown here on a 'Peveril' photographic postcard.

All Saints' Church. Nottm.

3. The interior of All Saints Church, Raleigh Street, Radford.

4. Radford Recreation Ground, with William Hollins' Mill on Garden Street in the background. 'Peveril' series postcard.

5. In 1920 there were seven window-blind makers in Nottingham, one of whom was T. Simmons Ltd. of Muggleston Yard and 107 Alfreton Road. This was one of his business postcards, sent to Kirkby-in-Ashfield in August 1920.

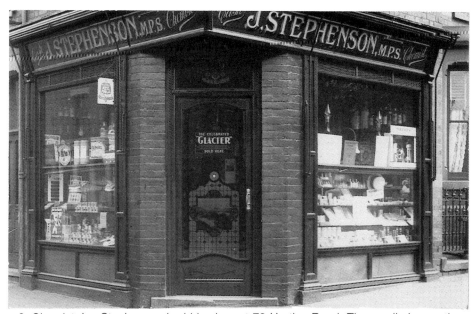

6. Chemist Jas Stephenson had his shop at 72 Hartley Road. The small sign on the left window – N.T.C. Public – indicates that telephone calls could be made by the public in the shop. Anonymously-published postcard from c.1920.

7. The chemist's shop of Wm. Holland was located on the corner of Independent Street and Alfreton Road, as seen on this postcard published about 1904. The shop was taken over in the 1920s by Jack Hutchby.

294 ALFRETON ROA

8. W.H. Smith published this card showing tramcar no.57 descending Alfreton Road.
Postal usage of May 1915 gives the clue to the date.

OTTINGHAM.

9. The "Portland Arms" (proprietor T. Wilson) on Portland Road off Alfreton Road in 1905 on a card published by Henson & Co. of Nottingham. Plenty of local children can be seen on this quiet street scene.

10. 'Peveril' series card showing the interior of the Wesleyan Methodist Chapel, De Leigne Street. *"Beautiful weather here: we are having a most enjoyable holiday"*, wrote 'Sis' to Miss Ethel Ogden of Bacup in June 1908.

11. An extremely smart class from the Norton Street Boys School pose for the photographer on 20th June 1919.

12. The 'Pierrots' at the Old Radford Flower Show sports on this c.1918 postcard by C.W. Marsh, West End Studios, 24 Moorgate Street, Radford.

13. The offices of John Player & Sons, Radford Boulevard, c.1906 on an anonymously-published card.

14. A later card of the same scene, published by C. & A.G. Lewis in 1923.

Player's Castle Tobacco Factory
Extensions. 17th August, 1912.

15. In 1912 Player's Castle Tobacco factory was extended, and this card shows some of the work in progress. The postcard was sent to Reading on 9th September of that year.

Player's Castle Tobacco Factory
Extensions. 17th August, 1912.

16. A similar card, showing extension work in progress in August 1912.

17. Members of the John Player Fire Brigade pose by their tender in 1913. The anonymously-published card was sent to Reading in October of that year.

PLAYER'S CASTLE TOBACCO FACTORY
NOTTINGHAM

18. A more recent aerial view of Player's Castle Tobacco Factory. The imposing structures are highlighted in this picture.

19. The visit of King George V and Queen Mary to Nottingham on 24th June 1914 included a stop at the John Player factory. The welcoming banner announces that 2,500 people were employed by the company.

20. The Prince of Wales (later Edward VIII) came to Nottingham on 11th July 1928, and once again Player's factory was part of the royal itinerary. 'Rex' series postcard.

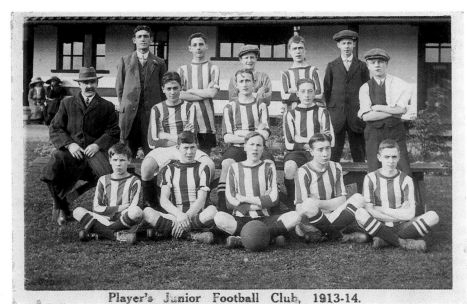

Player's Junior Football Club, 1913-14.

21. John Player's junior football team of 1913-14 pose on this photo taken and published as a postcard by B.C. Mann, 125 Norton Street, Radford.

22. Members of Norton Street Football Club on a card produced for club assistant secretary Eric Cooke in July 1938.

23. Radford railway station on the Midland connecting line from Nottingham to Trowell, which closed in October 1964. A c.1956 photograph by H.B. Priestley.

BOBBERS MILL—NOTTINGHAM

24. Bobbers Mill, Radford, on a 'Clumber' series postcard sent to Miss Mantle in Hyson Green. *"Another one for your collection"*, wrote the sender.

283   RADFORD ROAD. HYSON GREEN. NOTTINGHAM

25. Radford Road, Hyson Green, on a sunny day in 1910. The Union of London and Smith's Bank is in the right foreground. The postcard, published by W.H. Smith, shows a view looking down towards Gregory Boulevard.

26. A fine photograph on a card by C. & A.G. Lewis showing a scene looking up Radford Road toward Bentinck Road. The locally famous store of drapers and milliners, Staddon & Sons, is prominent on the right of the card.

27. The "Grand Theatre" on Radford Road pictured in 1906 on a 'Clumber' series postcard. The theatre itself was opened on 1st February 1886. 'The Sign of the Cross' was on offer, according to the poster on the side.

28. The corner of Radford Road and Gregory Boulevard seemed a reasonable place for these two women in the middle of the road to have a chat in this c.1922 scene on a C. & A.G. Lewis postcard. The only traffic hazard appears to be the wheeled basket to the right of the card, but a policeman is at hand to check out the situation. The police station can be seen on the left.

29. Radford Road just before the junction with Gregory
"Grand Theatre", with Beach's Boot Store on the corner o
in this 1923 view, but there are plenty of pedestrians abou

d on another Lewis card. Prominent on the left is the
ey Road. A tram and motor car make up the only fraffic

30. An anonymously-published card of the Nottingham and Notts Banking Co. Ltd., of 105 Radford Road, on the corner of Gregory Boulevard and Radford Road.

31. 'Peveril' postcard of 1905, featuring the Nottingham General Dispensary, standing next to the Public Library on Gregory Boulevard. The resident surgeon at the time was Miss Edith Woods.

32. Early transport outside F. Mitchell's garage at 110 Radford Road. This 'Peveril' series card was posted in November 1905 by Mr. Mitchell himself to 'Phil Jones, Esq., Coventry'. If that was the only address required, Mr. Jones must have been well-known in Coventry!

33. Another 'Peveril' card showing the police station on the corner of Radford Road and Gregory Boulevard *(see illus. 28)*. Tramcar no. 48 is on the Basford-Hyson Green-Market Place route.

34. Headmaster and staff of St. Paul's Church School, Hyson Green, prior to World War One.

35. Class II of the same school in 1913 on a card by F. Bostock of Nottingham.

36. St. Paul's Church in Hyson Green was built in 1843 at a cost of £3,900. The living in 1904 was worth £300 yearly. 'Peveril' series card, sent to Weston-on-Trent in September 1911.

37. This could well be one of the classes of the Scotholme School, Hyson Green. To judge by the children's dress, it probably dates from around 1910.

394   RADFORD

38. Radford Road, Hyson Green, on a W.H. Smith card of about 1914.

, NOTTINGHAM

39. This splendid group, posed on the corner of Cope Street and Palin Street, comprises the steam lorry, equipment, and staff of Thomas Gray, furniture removers, of 10 Palin Street, Hyson Green.

395   ST STEPHEN'S CHURCH, NOTTINGHAM

40. St. Stephens Church, Bobbers Mill Road, Hyson Green. W.H. Smith postcard, sent to Mansfield Woodhouse in September 1916.

41. Mr. W. Crane stands on the doorstep of his beer-off on Radford Road, Hyson Green. The card was posted in Bulwell in February 1906.

-28-

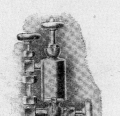

3.500/12-29 '907

SMITH BROTHERS & Co. (Hyson) Ltd.

ENGINEERS, IRON & BRASS FOUNDERS,

Telegraphic Address:
"HYSON, NOTTINGHAM."
Telephone 7234-5.

Hyson Green Valve Works, NOTTINGHAM.

....19

We Manufacture—

Pressure Gauges. Whistles & Syrens
Asbestos Packed Cocks.
Safety and Reducing Valves.
Ejectors and Injectors.
Cast Steel, Iron and G.M. Valves.
Oil Cups and Lubricators,
Radiator Fittings.

Specialists in Oil Valves up to 2,000 lbs. pressure

42. An advertising/business card for Smith Brothers of Bobbers Mill Road, Hyson Green. It was sent as an order acknowledgement to a firm in Newark in August 1930.

43. The Forest, showing the Racecourse Grandstand. The oval course, which had been closed in 1892, was 1¼ miles in length. The Grandstand itself was demolished in 1910.

44. Goose Fair moved to the Forest Recreation Ground in 1928 from the Market Square. This 'Rex' series card of c.1930 shows young children waiting for a ride on the 'Slip'.

45. Celebration on the Forest of King George V and Queen Mary's Coronation Day in June 1911. Card published by Gibson & Son.

Montgomery & Co   CHILDREN'S CORONATION DEMONSTRATION, THE FOREST, NOTTINGHAM   Nottingham

46. Large gathering of children on the Forest on that same day, seen on a card from Montgomery & Co. of Nottingham.

47. Five weeks before the outbreak of World War One, the King and Queen visited Nottingham *(see also illus. 19-20 and 55-6).* This card by Henson & Co. shows them being greeted by children on the Forest.

48. The Grandstand *(see illus. 43)* about 1906 from a different angle on a 'Clumber' series postcard. On the skyline in the distance is St. Andrews Church. It looks as though there's an interval rest during a serious game of cricket here!

49. An unusual card: two men on the Forest – about 1912 – with collecting boxes for the Nottingham Hospital.

50. Edwardian humour focusing on evening activity on Nottingham Forest. This is one of several featuring 'Nottinghamshire after dark' but could easily be overprinted with the names of other locations.

113   "THE TEST MATCH", THE FOREST, NOTTINGHAM.

51. More cricket: while the youngsters pose for the photographer, in the background a horse waits patiently, tethered to what appears to be a grass-cutting machine. W.H. Smith postcard, sent to France in July 1913.

215   BOWLING GREEN ON FOREST, NOTTINGHAM.

52. A fine array of headgear on the Forest Bowling Green about 1912. Another W.H. Smith card, sent to Leicester in August 1913.

120   THE FOREST, NOTTINGHAM.

53. Edwardian children in their Sunday best, out for a walk with mother or nanny, and seen on a W.H. Smith card which was posted to Sydenham in September 1910.

Nottingham Forest, from Bentinck. Rd

54. Many early postcards were cleverly animated by the photographer by judicious use of posing children, who would naturally be delighted to be featured. 'Clumber' series card showing the Forest from Bentinck Road.

55. An anonymously-published card showing Alberta Terrace decorated for the Royal Visit of 24th June 1914. The premises on the right are those of decorator H. Smith, and the photo was taken from Sherwood Rise.

56. A rare card of the same visit, showing the crowd on Alberta Terrace waiting for the royal couple after George and Mary had been to the Guy Birkin lace factory. Published by J. Henry Scott of Bulcote.